# Metals and Nonmetals

## by Daniel R. Faust

Consultant: Sara Vogt
Science Educator at Anoka Hennepin School District

**BEARPORT**
PUBLISHING

Minneapolis, Minnesota

## Bearport Publishing Company Product Development Team

President: Jen Jenson; Director of Product Development: Spencer Brinker; Senior Editor: Allison Juda; Editor: Charly Haley; Associate Editor: Naomi Reich; Senior Designer: Colin O'Dea; Associate Designer: Elena Klinkner; Associate Designer: Kayla Eggert; Product Development Assistant: Anita Stasson

Library of Congress Cataloging-in-Publication Data is available at www.loc.gov or upon request from the publisher.

ISBN: 979-8-88509-425-2 (hardcover)
ISBN: 979-8-88509-547-1 (paperback)
ISBN: 979-8-88509-662-1 (ebook)

For more information, write to Bearport Publishing, 5357 Penn Avenue South, Minneapolis, MN 55419.

# Contents

# All Around

The food you eat and the clothes you wear have something in common. So do your favorite devices. Almost everything around you is made of metals, nonmetals, or both. These two groups of **elements** make up many important things we use every day.

What is made of metal, and what is a nonmetal? Some things might surprise you. There are fabrics with metals woven into them.

Some athletic clothing has metal in it.

# A Place on the Table

Elements are the basic things that make up everything in this universe. There are 118 known elements. Each one has its own **properties**.

Scientists use these properties to organize the elements. They put the elements in order on the periodic table.

Elements on the periodic table are organized based on the parts of the elements and how they come together. This is similar to how you would find books of the same genre together in a library.

# The Periodic Table of Elements

| | | | | | | | | | | | | | | | | | |
|---|---|---|---|---|---|---|---|---|---|---|---|---|---|---|---|---|---|
| **1** H 1.008 Hydrogen | | | | | | | | | | | | | | | | | **2** He 4.002602 Helium |
| **3** Li 6.94 Lithium | **4** Be 9.0121831 Beryllium | | | | | | | | | | | **5** B 10.81 Boron | **6** C 12.011 Carbon | **7** N 14.007 Nitrogen | **8** O 15.999 Oxygen | **9** F 18.998403163 Fluorine | **10** Ne 20.1797 Neon |
| **11** Na 22.98976928 Sodium | **12** Mg 24.305 Magnesium | | | | | | | | | | | **13** Al 26.9815385 Aluminium | **14** Si 28.085 Silicon | **15** P 30.973761998 Phosphorus | **16** S 32.06 Sulfur | **17** Cl 35.45 Chlorine | **18** Ar 39.948 Argon |
| **19** K 39.0983 Potassium | **20** Ca 40.078 Calcium | **21** Sc 44.955908 Scandium | **22** Ti 47.867 Titanium | **23** V 50.9415 Vanadium | **24** Cr 51.9961 Chromium | **25** Mn 54.938044 Manganese | **26** Fe 55.845 Iron | **27** Co 58.933194 Cobalt | **28** Ni 58.6934 Nickel | **29** Cu 63.546 Copper | **30** Zn 65.38 Zinc | **31** Ga 69.723 Gallium | **32** Ge 72.630 Germanium | **33** As 74.921595 Arsenic | **34** Se 78.971 Selenium | **35** Br 79.904 Bromine | **36** Kr 83.798 Krypton |
| **37** Rb 85.4678 Rubidium | **38** Sr 87.62 Strontium | **39** Y 88.90584 Yttrium | **40** Zr 91.224 Zirconium | **41** Nb 92.90637 Niobium | **42** Mo 95.95 Molybdenum | **43** Tc 98 Technetium | **44** Ru 101.07 Ruthenium | **45** Rh 102.90550 Rhodium | **46** Pd 106.42 Palladium | **47** Ag 107.8682 Silver | **48** Cd 112.414 Cadmium | **49** In 114.818 Indium | **50** Sn 118.710 Tin | **51** Sb 121.760 Antimony | **52** Te 127.60 Tellurium | **53** I 126.90447 Iodine | **54** Xe 131.293 Xenon |
| **55** Cs 132.90545196 Caesium | **56** Ba 137.327 Barium | 57-71 | **72** Hf 178.49 Hafnium | **73** Ta 180.94788 Tantalum | **74** W 183.84 Tungsten | **75** Re 186.207 Rhenium | **76** Os 190.23 Osmium | **77** Ir 192.217 Iridium | **78** Pt 195.084 Platinum | **79** Au 196.966569 Gold | **80** Hg 200.592 Mercury | **81** Tl 204.38 Thallium | **82** Pb 207.2 Lead | **83** Bi 208.98040 Bismuth | **84** Po 209 Polonium | **85** At 210 Astatine | **86** Rn 222 Radon |
| **87** Fr 223 Francium | **88** Ra 226 Radium | 89-103 | **104** Rf 267 Rutherfordium | **105** Db 268 Dubnium | **106** Sg 269 Seaborgium | **107** Bh 270 Bohrium | **108** Hs 269 Hassium | **109** Mt 278 Meitnerium | **110** Ds 281 Darmstadtium | **111** Rg 281 Roentgenium | **112** Cn 285 Copernicium | **113** Nh 286 Nihonium | **114** Fl 289 Flerovium | **115** Mc 289 Moscovium | **116** Lv 293 Livermorium | **117** Ts 294 Tennessine | **118** Og 294 Oganesson |

| | | | | | | | | | | | | | | |
|---|---|---|---|---|---|---|---|---|---|---|---|---|---|---|
| **57** La 138.90547 Lanthanum | **58** Ce 140.116 Cerium | **59** Pr 140.90766 Praseodymium | **60** Nd 144.242 Neodymium | **61** Pm 145 Promethium | **62** Sm 150.36 Samarium | **63** Eu 151.964 Europium | **64** Gd 157.25 Gadolinium | **65** Tb 158.92535 Terbium | **66** Dy 162.500 Dysprosium | **67** Ho 164.93033 Holmium | **68** Er 167.259 Erbium | **69** Tm 168.93422 Thulium | **70** Yb 173.054 Ytterbium | **71** Lu 174.9668 Lutetium |
| **89** Ac 227 Actinium | **90** Th 232.0377 Thorium | **91** Pa 231.03588 Protactinium | **92** U 238.02891 Uranium | **93** Np 237 Neptunium | **94** Pu 244 Plutonium | **95** Am 243 Americium | **96** Cm 247 Curium | **97** Bk 247 Berkelium | **98** Cf 251 Californium | **99** Es 252 Einsteinium | **100** Fm 257 Fermium | **101** Md 258 Mendelevium | **102** No 259 Nobelium | **103** Lr 266 Lawrencium |

Dmitri Mendeleev made the first periodic table in 1869.

The largest groups of elements are metals and nonmetals. Metals can be found on the left side of the periodic table. Most nonmetal elements are on the right. Metal and nonmetal elements can be broken into smaller categories, too.

The periodic table has 7 rows and 18 columns. The rows are periods. The columns are called groups or families. Elements within each period and family share things in common.

# Metals and Nonmetals

**A family**

**A period**

| 1 H 1.008 Hydrogen | | | | | | | | | | | | | | | | | 2 He 4.002602 Helium |
|---|---|---|---|---|---|---|---|---|---|---|---|---|---|---|---|---|---|
| 3 Li 6.94 Lithium | 4 Be 9.0121831 Beryllium | | | | | | | | | | | 5 B 10.81 Boron | 6 C 12.011 Carbon | 7 N 14.007 Nitrogen | 8 O 15.999 Oxygen | 9 F 18.998403163 Fluorine | 10 Ne 20.1797 Neon |
| 11 Na 22.98976928 Sodium | 12 Mg 24.305 Magnesium | | | | | | | | | | | 13 Al 26.9815385 Aluminium | 14 Si 28.085 Silicon | 15 P 30.973761998 Phosphorus | 16 S 32.06 Sulfur | 17 Cl 35.45 Chlorine | 18 Ar 39.948 Argon |
| 19 K 39.0983 Potassium | 20 Ca 40.078 Calcium | 21 Sc 44.955908 Scandium | 22 Ti 47.867 Titanium | 23 V 50.9415 Vanadium | 24 Cr 51.9961 Chromium | 25 Mn 54.938044 Manganese | 26 Fe 55.845 Iron | 27 Co 58.933194 Cobalt | 28 Ni 58.6934 Nickel | 29 Cu 63.546 Copper | 30 Zn 65.38 Zinc | 31 Ga 69.723 Gallium | 32 Ge 72.630 Germanium | 33 As 74.921595 Arsenic | 34 Se 78.971 Selenium | 35 Br 79.904 Bromine | 36 Kr 83.798 Krypton |
| 37 Rb 85.4678 Rubidium | 38 Sr 87.62 Strontium | 39 Y 88.90584 Yttrium | 40 Zr 91.224 Zirconium | 41 Nb 92.90637 Niobium | 42 Mo 95.95 Molybdenum | 43 Tc 98 Technetium | 44 Ru 101.07 Ruthenium | 45 Rh 102.90550 Rhodium | 46 Pd 106.42 Palladium | 47 Ag 107.8682 Silver | 48 Cd 112.414 Cadmium | 49 In 114.818 Indium | 50 Sn 118.710 Tin | 51 Sb 121.760 Antimony | 52 Te 127.60 Tellurium | 53 I 126.90447 Iodine | 54 Xe 131.293 Xenon |
| 55 Cs 132.90545196 Caesium | 56 Ba 137.327 Barium | 57-71 | 72 Hf 178.49 Hafnium | 73 Ta 180.94788 Tantalum | 74 W 183.84 Tungsten | 75 Re 186.207 Rhenium | 76 Os 190.23 Osmium | 77 Ir 192.217 Iridium | 78 Pt 195.084 Platinum | 79 Au 196.966569 Gold | 80 Hg 200.592 Mercury | 81 Tl 204.38 Thallium | 82 Pb 207.2 Lead | 83 Bi 208.98040 Bismuth | 84 Po 209 Polonium | 85 At 210 Astatine | 86 Rn 222 Radon |
| 87 Fr 223 Francium | 88 Ra 226 Radium | 89-103 | 104 Rf 267 Rutherfordium | 105 Db 268 Dubnium | 106 Sg 269 Seaborgium | 107 Bh 270 Bohrium | 108 Hs 269 Hassium | 109 Mt 278 Meitnerium | 110 Ds 281 Darmstadtium | 111 Rg 281 Roentgenium | 112 Cn 285 Copernicium | 113 Nh 286 Nihonium | 114 Fl 289 Flerovium | 115 Mc 289 Moscovium | 116 Lv 293 Livermorium | 117 Ts 294 Tennessine | 118 Og 294 Oganesson |

| 57 La 138.90547 Lanthanum | 58 Ce 140.116 Cerium | 59 Pr 140.90766 Praseodymium | 60 Nd 144.242 Neodymium | 61 Pm 145 Promethium | 62 Sm 150.36 Samarium | 63 Eu 151.964 Europium | 64 Gd 157.25 Gadolinium | 65 Tb 158.92535 Terbium | 66 Dy 162.500 Dysprosium | 67 Ho 164.93033 Holmium | 68 Er 167.259 Erbium | 69 Tm 168.93422 Thulium | 70 Yb 173.054 Ytterbium | 71 Lu 174.9668 Lutetium |
|---|---|---|---|---|---|---|---|---|---|---|---|---|---|---|
| 89 Ac 227 Actinium | 90 Th 232.0377 Thorium | 91 Pa 231.03588 Protactinium | 92 U 238.02891 Uranium | 93 Np 237 Neptunium | 94 Pu 244 Plutonium | 95 Am 243 Americium | 96 Cm 247 Curium | 97 Bk 247 Berkelium | 98 Cf 251 Californium | 99 Es 252 Einsteinium | 100 Fm 257 Fermium | 101 Md 258 Mendelevium | 102 No 259 Nobelium | 103 Lr 266 Lawrencium |

☐ Metals    ☐ Nonmetals

**Sulfur is a nonmetal.**

**Magnesium is a metal.**

# What Makes It Metal?

Most of the known elements are metals. What are some of their properties? Almost all of these elements are solid at room temperature. They tend to be very **dense**, too. This means the parts that make up these elements are packed together tightly.

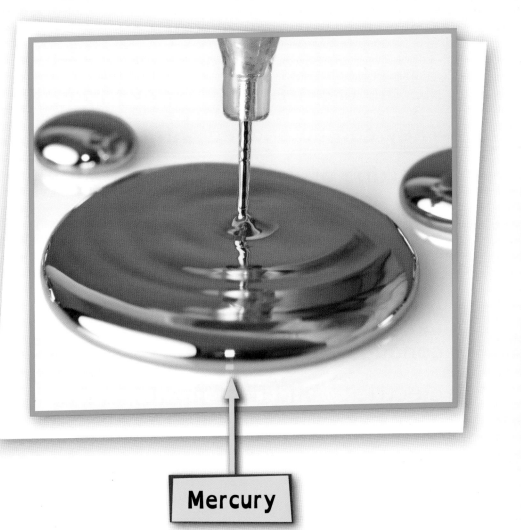

**Mercury**

It takes a lot of energy to make most metals melt. Some can even stay solid in the heat of a wood fire. Mercury is an exception. It is the only known metal that is liquid at room temperature.

Metals are often hard and strong. They can be shaped without breaking or cracking. Metals hold their shapes until they are made into something new.

Many metals are also good **conductors**. This means electricity and heat move through them easily.

One of the easiest ways to guess whether an element is a metal is by looking at it. Most metals are shiny.

Because they are shiny and easy to shape, metals are often made into jewelry.

# Making from Metals

The properties of metals make them useful for many things. They are used to make cookware. It's easy to fry an egg on a pan that conducts heat. Being easy to bend and carrying electricity well make some metals perfect for electrical wiring.

Copper and aluminum are the most common metals used for electrical wiring. Silver is good at conducting electricity. However, it is harder to bend and costs much more. This means it is used less often.

Aluminum is common in cookware.

Copper is often used for electrical wiring.

A metal can be combined with another element to form an **alloy**. Often, this is done to get the best properties of both elements. When iron is combined with another element, such as carbon, it makes the **synthetic** material steel. Steel is easy to shape like the metal iron, but it is stronger.

What other alloys have you seen? A bronze third-place medal is made of mixed metals. So is the brass used in many musical instruments.

Steel

# When It's Not Metal

Elements that do not have the properties of metals are nonmetals. There are fewer nonmetals than metals. Nonmetal elements are not as similar to one another as metals. However, nonmetals that share properties are near one another on the periodic table.

One group of nonmetals is called noble gases. These elements have many uses. Helium can make balloons float. Argon, krypton, and neon are used in lighting.

# Know Your Nonmetals

Many nonmetals have a low **boiling point**. This is the temperature at which they go from liquid to gas. Because of this, many nonmetals are gases at room temperature.

Even as solids, nonmetals have different properties than metals. They are **brittle**. This makes it harder to shape nonmetals.

What else do nonmetals have in common? They do not have the properties of metals! Most nonmetals do not look shiny. They are rarely good conductors.

Chlorine is a gas at room temperature.

# Important Elements

Depending on their properties, nonmetals are used for many important things. Plants and animals could not survive without the nonmetal elements oxygen, carbon, and hydrogen. Many of the **nutrients** our bodies need are nonmetals, too. Nonmetals are even used to make different kinds of medicines, soaps, and plastics.

There may be fewer of them, but nonmetals are everywhere. Oxygen is the most common element on Earth. About 20 percent of the air around the planet is oxygen.

# Crossing the Line

Some elements have properties of both metals and nonmetals. They are called metalloids. Metalloids usually look like metals but have other properties of nonmetals. For example, they aren't good conductors. Metalloids can be found on the periodic table between most of the metals and nonmetals.

Silicon is a metalloid that is found in most kinds of rock. It is used to make concrete and glass. The element is also found in rubber.

# Metalloids

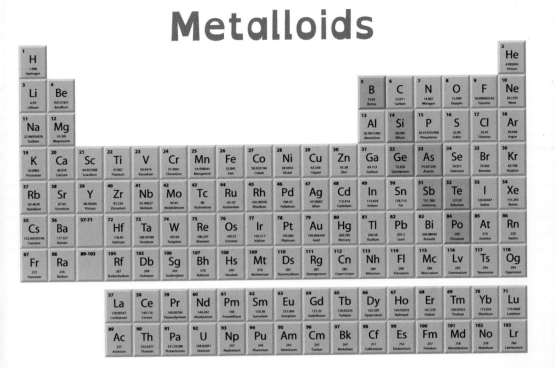

Metalloids

Silicon

# Under Our Feet

We're willing to go to the ends of the earth for the important elements we use every day . . . literally. We dig deep underground to find many of these metals, nonmetals, and metalloids. Can you imagine life on Earth without what's buried under your feet?

Earth's elements are limited. What will we do when we run out? Some people have suggested we look to space. One day, we might visit other planets to get the elements we need.

# Metals, Nonmetals, and Metalloids

Metals and nonmetals have different properties. What can you expect from elements in each group?

| METALS | • Mostly solid at room temperature<br>• Dense<br>• Hard and strong<br>• Easily shaped<br>• Good conductors<br>• Shiny | Copper |
|---|---|---|
| NONMETALS | • Often gas at room temperature<br>• Brittle as solid<br>• Difficult to shape<br>• Not shiny<br>• Not good conductors | Helium |
| METALLOIDS | • Often solid at room temperature<br>• Often shiny<br>• Not good conductors | Silicon |

## ★ SilverTips for REVIEW

Review what you've learned. Use the text to help you.

### Define key terms

metal

metalloid

nonmetal

periodic table

property

### Check for understanding

What are some of the common properties of metals?

How are metals and nonmetals different?

Name two uses for metals and two uses for nonmetals. What about their properties makes them good for these things?

### Think deeper

Thinking of your daily life, what are some of the most common things you use? Based on their properties, do you think they are metals, nonmetals, or metalloids?

## ★ SilverTips on TEST-TAKING

- **Make a study plan.** Ask your teacher what the test is going to cover. Then, set aside time to study a little bit every day.

- **Read all the questions carefully.** Be sure you know what is being asked.

- **Skip any questions** you don't know how to answer right away. Mark them and come back later if you have time.

# Glossary

**alloy** something made from a metal element mixed with one or more other elements

**boiling point** the temperature at which something goes from a liquid to a gas

**brittle** hard but easily broken or cracked

**conductors** materials that allow heat or electricity to move through them

**dense** with things packed closely together

**elements** any of the more than 100 substances that cannot be broken down into simpler substances

**nutrients** substances that plants and animals need to live and grow

**properties** the ways things look or act

**synthetic** made by humans rather than nature

# Read More

O'Mara, Kennon. *Elements (A Look at Chemistry)*. New York: Gareth Stevens, 2019.

Petersen, Christine. *Explore Ores (Geology Rocks!)*. Minneapolis: Abdo Publishing, 2020.

Thomas, Isabel. *Exploring the Elements: A Complete Guide to the Periodic Table*. New York: Phaidon Press, 2021.

# Learn More Online

1. Go to **www.factsurfer.com** or scan the QR code below.

2. Enter "**Metals and Nonmetals**" into the search box.

3. Click on the cover of this book to see a list of websites.

# Index

# About the Author

Daniel R. Faust is a freelance writer of fiction and nonfiction. He lives in Brooklyn, NY.